# Tiger Chinese Horoscope 2025

By
IChingHunFùyǒu FengShuisu

# Table of Contents

# Introduce

## The character of people born in the year of the TIGER

You are a brave, fearless, competitive individual who is willing to go through both your brains and the force. Because you are optimistic, a leader, and intelligent, people are drawn to you. Tigers are generous, but if they are bullied, they will become scolded and violent. In terms of work and finances, the tiger was born to be the lord of the jungle, with its kingdom deep within, so you don't like being a subordinate, money isn't a big deal, and prestige is more important, even if it's difficult to achieve. You will not submit to someone you do not respect. If you work and your boss does not respect you, you will resign and look for another job immediately.

You are not a greedy person who enjoys collecting money and living a comfortable life in which happiness is always available. There is no need to work hard and then spend money on happiness to compensate later. You're always generous to your friends, but if someone doesn't talk to your ears, you'll lose them. You're also ready to smoke out of your ears if a long-term partner knows you're easily irritated and recover quickly. Your new friends, on the other hand, will be taken aback. Nothing at all. You take love seriously. Love someone who truly loves you, but quickly grows bored and enters love textbooks, and when you break up, you can find someone new very quickly.

**Strength:**
Others admire you for your willingness to assist others.

**Weaknesses:**
You are as impatient as a tiger and refuse to listen to anyone who encourages you to hurt yourself.

**Love:**
The majority of Tigers are very people who enjoy allowing others to love themselves. People born in this year are often very selective and do not have a particular love for anyone.

They sometimes choose too many things until they have nothing left. However, with charming words, some easily fall in love with the Tiger. If you think you're going to deceive, you'll have to plan carefully because people born this year are very smart. Because you're constantly meeting new people, it's easy to fall in love with people from all over.

**Suitable Career:**
Planting trees, landscaping, making wooden furniture, trading wood, selling flowers, and stationery, selling books, publishing, printing houses, selling paper, novelists, teachers, opening a pharmacy, selling tea leaves, or occupations related to herbs such as selling cosmetics with herbs as an ingredient, making spas, selling fabrics, plastics, or equipment related to worshiping gods or telecom And businesses involving import-export, dealing with foreigners, and so on are all appropriate for those born in the year of the Tiger.

## Year of the TIGER (Wood) | (1950) & (2010)

"The TIGER descending the mountain " is a person born in the year of the TIGER at the age of 75 years (1950) and 15 years (2010)

## Overview

For senior people in this age group, this year you will have a smooth life. Your life will change for the better. Whatever you think or do, you will have someone to support you. Therefore, in terms of business and trade, you should transfer it to your children. You should find happiness by choosing to do activities that you like to relax your mind. However, because in your horoscope, there is an evil star "Tiew Kae" that is harassing you, this year you must be careful about health problems. Slipping and falling and accidents will result in injuries and bleeding. In addition, the family is likely to be in mourning. At the beginning of the year, you should find time to worship the gods and deities and pray to the god Tai Sui to ask for his blessing to protect you from bad things and to reduce the conflicting power. Ask for blessings to not get sick and for your family to be peaceful and happy. For young people, this year your studies and exams are overall good and progressing. For some people, you will have the opportunity to apply for a new school or may be able to study abroad. But if it is during the 4th Chinese month (5 May – 4 June), 5th Chinese month (5 June – 6 July), 9th Chinese month (8 October – 6 November), and 11th Chinese month (7 December 2025 – 4 January 2026), you must be careful of accidents and following your friends' invitations to go in the direction of vices or joining groups to do activities that go astray. It may drag you into trouble and destroy your future. Therefore, please use your mind to consider carefully. And since your birth year is classified as another unlucky zodiac sign, at the beginning of the year you should find an opportunity to pay respect to the Tai Sui deity to relieve the bad luck from being heavy and make it lighter.

## Career and Business

For the teenage horoscope, even though the horoscope has the stars supporting and supporting, and some adults are advisors and helpers, resulting in the progress in the study direction, However, this year is still a year that you should persevere and study hard because in the end, you are your refuge, so you will have sustainable progress.

The months when both your career and study of the horoscope in both cycles of life will be easily obstructed and problematic are the 4th Chinese month (May 5 - June 4), the 5th Chinese month (June 5 - July 6), the 9th Chinese month (October 8 - November 6), and the 11th Chinese month (December 7, 68 - January 4, 69). During this period, be careful about making various contracts. You should consider the terms and conditions to see if they will cause problems later. When starting a new job, investing in shares or various investments, be careful of being cheated in accounting, and there may be a problem of capital leakage or many obstacles and problems. Therefore, it is better to avoid investing during this period for peace of mind. The months in which your work and studies will change for the better are the 2nd Chinese month (5 March – 3 April), the 6th Chinese month (7 July – 6 August), the 8th Chinese month (7 September – 7 October) and the 10th Chinese month (7 November – 6 December).

**Financial**

The finances of both horoscopes this year are in chaos. They will lose money from medical expenses and other damages. In particular, the lack of liquidity will make you tired of managing to balance your income and expenses. Therefore, this year you should spend thriftily and plan your finances well from the beginning of the year.

You should not lend money to others or guarantee for anyone to reduce losses. Especially during the months when your finances are in stagnation and low, namely the 4th Chinese month (May 5 - June 4), the 5th Chinese month (June 5 - July 6), the 9th Chinese month (October 8 - November 6), and the 11th Chinese month (December 7, 2025 - January 4, 2026). You should avoid all types of risky investments, including gambling and taking risks. You should also not invest or get involved in businesses that are likely to be illegal. Otherwise, it will hurt you and your family.

For the months with bright financial fortune, they are the 2nd Chinese month (5 March – 3 April), the 6th Chinese month (7 July – 6 August), the 8th Chinese month (7 September – 7 October) and the 10th Chinese month (7 November – 6 December).

## Family

This year, your family will not be peaceful. This is because of the influence of the evil stars, which will cause arguments and turn small things into big issues, causing a lack of peace in your home. In particular, the months when your family will easily encounter problems and conflicts are the  4th Chinese month (May 5 – June 4), the 5th Chinese month (June 5 – July 6), the 9th Chinese month (October 8 – November 6), and the 11th Chinese month (December 7, 2025 – January 4, 2026). Be careful of accidents and take care of the health of the elderly in your home more closely. Be careful of arguments between insiders and outsiders that will cause chaos and trouble. Be careful of scams from criminals. There is also a chance that you will suffer and have to mourn for your elders.

For teenagers, this year is a moderate chance because the auspicious star Tian-Ik will orbit to help strengthen your relationships and you will find friends who will help you with your studies, which will help you progress even further. However, it also depends on you, the person who has the horoscope, to know how to choose who to hang out with. Don't forget to hang out with good friends. It will also lead you to good things.

**Love**
The overall love situation for both horoscopes this year is quite smooth. For the elders, if they are not involved with people around them too much, the care and respect from children and grandchildren is still good as usual. However, during the 4th Chinese month (May 5 - June 4), the 5th Chinese month (June 5 - July 6), the 9th Chinese month (October 8 - November 6), and the 11th Chinese month (December 7, 2025 -

January 4, 2026), the horoscope should be careful with words because they may cause arguments in the house. As for the young horoscopes during these months, they should carefully consider who comes as a friend or who has other hidden motives. Especially women, do not fall for sweet words because you may be deceived and hurt. Love should take time to study and learn about each other. The road is still long. Both of you must help each other and support each other in a good way. Gradually develop the relationship. This will help your love tree bloom and bear beautiful fruit.

## Health

This year, the health of the elderly is not very good. They tend to get sick sometimes. Three days are good, four days are always feverish. In addition, they must be careful of gastritis, intestinal diseases, dry mouth and throat, and new and old complications will come to visit. Therefore, they should be more strict about taking care of themselves, both exercising and eating healthy food. Including taking tonics and regularly seeing a doctor as scheduled, especially during the 4th Chinese month (May 5 - June 4), the 5th Chinese month (June 5 - July 6), the 9th Chinese month (October 8 - November 6), and the 11th Chinese month (December 7, 2025 - January 4, 2026). The elderly must be careful of getting sick and having to be hospitalized for a long time. As for the health of the young people, during these months, they should be careful of accidents from various activities, including traveling, which will result in injuries and bleeding, especially injuries to the legs.

## Year of the TIGER (Golden) | (1962)

" The TIGER walks in the forest " is a person born in the year of the TIGER at the age of 63 years (1962)


## Overview

For people with horoscopes in this age group, since your birth year is considered a year of conflict in the year of the Snake 2025, even though auspicious stars are moving in the zodiac, in your horoscope there are also evil stars of funeral guests staring and harassing you. Therefore, many activities that will proceed will not go as smoothly as you wish. Your work, including business, will encounter obstacles and problems. You will have to constantly work and fix them without stopping. However, this year, you should not let other people's words influence you to lose your identity. Every activity should have a clear goal and follow it. Do not be shaken by criticism.

In addition, work must be consistent and very determined. In addition, some activities require you to seize the opportunity. You must hurry up and do it. It is better than letting a good opportunity pass you by, which would be a pity. There is something important that the elderly should pay special attention to this year, which is unexpected events that may occur, especially your safety and the health of your family members. Because in the conflict year, there is always a chance for changes.

Therefore, it is better to be careful in every activity. If there is an auspicious event in your house this year, it will help alleviate the bad luck. But if there is no auspicious event, please be more careful. Do not be careless at all. At the beginning of the year, you should find time to worship the gods and deities, worship the Tai Sui deity to relieve misfortune, and ask for a happy life and the fulfillment of your wishes.

**Career and Business**

For this year's work and business, you must be patient and self-reliant. Even if there are patrons who offer to help, it seems that they will not be able to help to the fullest. It's like there is a lot of fire but little water, and the water is far away. It will take a long time to reach the fire. However, you should not expect anyone to help. In handling various matters, you will have to use immediate problem-solving and build friendships with people around you. Even if you get a small amount of water, it will help to reduce the severity. The months when your work horoscope is quite low and you will encounter many obstacles are the 4th Chinese month (May 5 - June 4), the 5th Chinese month (June 5 - July 6), the 9th Chinese month (October 8 - November 6), and the 11th Chinese month (December 7, 2025 - January 4, 2026). During this period, please do not interfere with other people's work. When drafting documents or contracts, be careful of conditions that hide details and take advantage. Including entering into shares, starting a new job, or investing in various things. This year, you will have to be extra careful. Although some items will receive benefits and dividends as targeted, many items will be deceived and lose money. The months in which your work will change direction for the better are the 2nd Chinese month (5 March – 3 April), the 6th

Chinese month (7 July – 6 August), the 8th Chinese month (7 September – 7 October) and the 10th Chinese month (7 November – 6 December).

## Financial

This year, your finances are in a state of losing money. There will be many unexpected expenses. Both the expenses that come in seem to exceed your income. Therefore, you should save anything you can to avoid falling into a crisis and lacking liquidity. Especially during the months when your finances are low and you will easily encounter problems, such as the 4th Chinese month (May 5 – June 4), the 5th Chinese month (June 5 – July 6), the 9th Chinese month (October 8 – November 6), and the 11th Chinese month (December 7, 2025 – January 4, 2026). Do not lend money to others. Do not sign financial guarantees. Do not gamble and take risks. Do not be greedy for wealth that does not belong to you. Be careful of investments during this period as you may be deceived. Also, do not invest in illegal businesses. The months when your finances flow smoothly are the 2nd

Chinese month (5 March – 3 April), the 6th Chinese month (7 July – 6 August), the 8th Chinese month (7 September – 7 October) and the 10th Chinese month (7 November – 6 December).

**Family**

Your family's destiny this year is not smooth due to the influence of the evil star Tiew Kaew who is harassing you. Therefore, please be careful of the unexpected and be careful of the safety of family members who may get injured, especially during the unlucky months such as the 4th Chinese month (May 5 - June 4), the 5th Chinese month (June 5 - July 6), the 9th Chinese month (October 8 - November 6), and the 11th Chinese month (December 7, 2025 - January 4, 2026), when you should be extra careful. If there is an auspicious event in the house, it will help to lighten the situation from serious to light. However, if there is no event, be careful of juniors or servants causing trouble. While working and traveling, you must be careful of accidents. In addition, be careful of conflicts within the house and mourning for elders. Also, do not get involved in conflicts between friends. Be careful that friends will betray you and cause you misfortune. It would be better to try to avoid having friends who have untrustworthy behaviors.

**Love**

This year, in terms of love and relationships, you should be careful of unexpected storms that may strike. Therefore, you should be careful not to be easily influenced by gossip and slander, and be careful that disagreements may turn into big conflicts. In addition, you should be careful with your own words and coldness, as well as less attention to your partner than usual, which will lead to arguments and quarrels, especially during the 4th Chinese Month (May 5 – June 4), the 5th Chinese Month (June 5 – July 6), the 9th Chinese month (October 8 – November 6), and the 11th Chinese Month (December 7, 2025 – January 4, 2026). During these periods, you should avoid getting involved with other people's families. Be careful that arguing will turn into bigger conflicts, and you should avoid going to entertainment venues because you may bring back sickness.

## Health

This year, you cannot be careless about your health. There is a chance that you will encounter unexpected disasters that may cause injuries or bleeding. Therefore, whether you are working traveling, or driving, you should be extra careful. Also, be careful of food poisoning, high blood pressure, liver disease, accumulated diseases caused by overeating, back pain, joint pain, and latent diseases that may appear. Especially in the 4th Chinese month (May 5 - June 4), the 5th Chinese month (June 5 - July 6), the 9th Chinese month (October 8 - November 6), and the 11th Chinese month (December 7, 2025 - January 4, 2026), you should pay special attention to any abnormalities in your body. If you have any problems, you should see a doctor for a detailed diagnosis. Do not let them spread or they will be difficult to treat. Exercise lightly and take care of your health to stay strong at all times.

## Year of the TIGER (Water) | (1974)

" The Tiger Takes a Stand" is a person born in the year of the TIGER at the age of 51 years (1974)

## Overview

For those born in the year of the Tiger, this year, because your birth year receives some conflicting power from the year of the Snake 2025, various inconveniences will come to your doorstep. Even though auspicious constellations are orbiting the same house of destiny, you cannot underestimate the inauspicious stars which will cause damage in many aspects. Both work and business will often encounter obstacles. Therefore, you cannot be impatient and careless in carrying out various activities this year because it may cause you to lose your work. If you need to fix something quickly, you should do it quickly because if you leave it for too long, it will be damaged beyond repair. Also, finances are important. There will be frequent unnecessary leakages and losses. Do not let debtors' accounts be collected for too long because they will be difficult to collect and may become bad debts. Do not spend extravagantly. Do not wait until you are in need before blaming yourself for not being extravagant. Furthermore, stress is also important. If you are too stressed, it will lead to serious illnesses. Therefore, you should relax by doing activities that you like, exercising, and getting enough rest. When you get enough sleep, your work will be efficient. You will gain wisdom and concentration in solving problems and this will help you survive the crisis. Things that you should pay attention to this year are The health of the elderly in the house who will get sick, causing loss of money with medical expenses, and must be careful of unexpected events in the house that cause chaos.

As for love, this year you should help each other to support each other so that the relationship that you have built together does not collapse. Therefore, when thinking of doing anything this year, in addition to using your mindfulness and caution, you must also always consider safety as your number one priority. Because the

Tiger zodiac in the Snake zodiac is considered to be another unlucky zodiac sign, so at the beginning of the year you should find time to worship and ward off bad luck to the Tai Sui deity to help you escape from crises and disasters, and ease heavy matters into light ones.

## Career and Business

This year, your career will face challenges. You should prepare yourself in every aspect to cope with unexpected situations. Therefore, when thinking of doing something, do not be impatient. You should do your best and strengthen good relationships with people around you who you have to contact. Make friends so that you have the opportunity to ask for help. This year, you should be careful with various investments. You should observe the situation calmly and clearly because this year, there is a chance of unpredictable fluctuations. If you enter the wrong market, the wrong person, or the wrong time, you will get hurt and lose your money. Especially during the unlucky months, which are the 4th Chinese month (May

5 - June 4), the 5th Chinese month (June 5 - July 6), the 9th Chinese month (October 8 - November 6), and the 11th Chinese month (December 7, 68 - January 4, 69). Be careful of protests by people in the store or organization. Be careful of signing work contracts that are not checked. You will be taken advantage of later.

For the months when your career has a chance to change for the better Including doing business that goes smoothly and efficiently, namely the 2nd Chinese month (5 March - 3 April), the 6th Chinese month (7 July - 6 August), the 8th Chinese month (7 September - 7 October) and the 10th Chinese month (7 November - 6 December). During the aforementioned period, joint ventures, starting new jobs, and investing in various areas will have a bright direction. Some channels or new businesses will have the opportunity to open and will see good profits and responses.

## Financial

This year's fortune is considered moderate. During the year, there may be a lack of liquidity in working capital. Therefore, there should be an emergency plan. Do not spend extravagantly on unnecessary things. Do not gamble or take risks. Do not be greedy. Beware of scammers, especially during the months when finances will be low and sluggish, which are the 4th Chinese month (May 5 - June 4), the 5th Chinese month (June 5 - July 6), the 9th Chinese month (October 8 - November 6), and the 11th Chinese month (December 7, 2025 - January 4, 2026). Do not lend money to others or be a financial guarantee. Be careful of unexpected expenses. Do not invest in illegal or immoral businesses. The months when your finances will flow smoothly are the 2nd Chinese month (5 March – 3 April), the 6th Chinese month (7 July – 6 August), the 8th Chinese month (7 September – 7 October) and the 10th Chinese month (7 November – 6 December).

**Family**

Due to the influence of the evil stars that dominate the horoscope, the family horoscope is not smooth. The horoscope owner should pay more attention to the safety of the family members, especially the elderly in the house. Be careful of accidents that will cause injuries and loss of property. Be careful of thieves, as well as arguments with family members. And be careful of unexpected events that will cause chaos and trouble for the whole family, especially during the 4th Chinese month (May 5 - June 4), the 5th Chinese month (June 5 - July 6), the 9th Chinese month (October 8 - November 6), and the 11th Chinese month (December 7, 68 - January 4, 69). Therefore, at the beginning of the year, you should find an opportunity to make merit and invite family members to make merit together. It may be better to go to the temple to offer alms or invite monks to chant at home. And should go to worship the gods and ask for blessings, especially worship the Tai Sui deity to avert bad luck and strengthen the horoscope to create peace and happiness for the whole family.

**Love**

This year, you will encounter both good and bad things. Even though you will be well taken care of by your partner, you may be attacked due to jealousy, which may be caused by yourself, who may be insatiable or not satisfied, or it may be karma from being led astray by others, which will lead to a family rift. Therefore, you should be mindful, have a restrained mind, and know right from wrong, so that you can support your family to be warm and happy, especially in the 4th Chinese month (May 5 - June 4), the 5th Chinese month (June 5 - July 6), the 9th Chinese month (October 8 - November 6), and the 11th Chinese month (December 7, 2025 - January 4, 2026). Do not get involved in other people's families. Be careful of arguments that may escalate into big problems. You should also avoid going to entertainment venues because they will bring suffering and trouble.

## Health

This year, the person will likely get sick easily, especially in the 4th Chinese month (May 5 – June 4), the 5th Chinese month (June 5 – July 6), the 9th Chinese month (October 8 – November 6), and the 11th Chinese month (December 7, 2025 – January 4, 2026). Therefore, you should take care of your hygiene, eat hygienic food, and be careful of diseases related to the digestive system, such as gastritis, infectious diseases, food poisoning, and liver disease. During travel, be careful of accidents that cause injuries or bleeding. In addition, you should get enough rest, do not be too stressed or overworked with work. You should let go sometimes. You should also find time to go on a vacation with your lover or family because, in addition to resting, it will also help promote family relationships. In addition, you should find time to exercise regularly. Avoid vices such as alcohol and cigarettes.

## Year of the TIGER (Wood) | (1986)

" The Tiger in the Jungle" is a person born in the year of the TIGER at the age of 39 years (1986)

## Overview

For those born in the year of the Tiger, this age group, when coming to the year of the Snake 2025, is classified as another zodiac sign that is in conflict. Therefore, bad energy covers the horoscope house. In addition, there will be a group of evil stars orbiting to disturb and spread influence. Which will result in conflicts and arguments easily. Duties and businesses will have problems and chaos. Unable to take care of everything at once. Also, subordinates will cause trouble. Therefore, for every activity this year, you should look carefully before doing it. Also, you should not interfere with other people's work. In addition, there is an important thing to be careful and control your manners and behavior, both gestures, actions, and words. Sometimes you express it without thinking, but other people may see and feel that you are sarcastic or belittling them, causing the other party to hold a grudge and unknowingly create an enemy. Sometimes, it is safer to speak less, meaning not saying everything you think. In addition, what you cannot neglect is the safety of your family members. Be careful of the health of people in the house, both the elderly and children. Also, this year you have a chance to mourn for an elder relative. However, the heavenly stars will help alleviate some of it. But another part depends on each person's karma. Therefore, at the beginning of the year, for many things to go smoothly, People with horoscopes should find time to worship the gods and deities and pray to the deity Tai Sui to avert bad luck and alleviate disasters. When you think well and act well, you will receive good things in return. In addition, the god will protect you and help reduce accidents and disasters, making them less severe.

## Career and Business

This year, even though your business is full of obstacles and problems, there are some periods of progress and prosperity. Therefore, you must increase your determination to work, and always develop your knowledge and skills, then you will see tangible results or increased income. However, you must work honestly, as the saying goes, "Honesty doesn't last long, but dishonesty doesn't last long." Because if the other party finds out, it means that your accumulated reputation will collapse right before your eyes. In addition, you should communicate clearly in your work so that the results will not be repeated mistakes that become a serious problem. Especially during the months when your work will be hindered and have many obstacles, namely, the 4th Chinese month (May 5 – June 4), the 5th Chinese month (June 5 – July 6), the 9th Chinese month (October 8 – November 6), and the 11th Chinese month (December 7, 2025 – January 4, 2026). Be careful not to be deceived when working during these periods. Also, when signing any contracts related to work, you should be patient and check carefully before signing. In particular, the months when your work and investments will have a good direction are the 2nd Chinese month ( March 5 – April 3), the 6th Chinese month ( July 7 – August 6), the 8th Chinese month (September 7

– October 7 ) and the 10th Chinese month ( November 7 – December 6).

**Financial**

This year, your financial horoscope is considered to be equal to your expenses. That is, even though you will have a beautiful income flowing in, there will be a lot of current expenses waiting. Therefore, you should be frugal, and allocate some for investment and some for savings so that you will have reserve money in case of emergency. The months when your financial luck is low and you should be careful with your spending are the 4th Chinese month (May 5 – June 4), the 5th Chinese month (June 5 – July 6), the 9th Chinese month (October 8 – November 6), and the 11th Chinese month (December 7, 2025 – January 4, 2026). During this period, you should not lend money to others or be a guarantor on behalf of others. Do not be greedy or you will easily fall prey to fraudsters. You should also avoid getting involved in businesses that are likely to be illegal, as this will cause trouble and danger. The months when your finances will be smooth and bright are the 2nd Chinese month (5 March – 3 April), the 6th Chinese month ( July 7 – August 6), the 8th Chinese month ( September 7 – October 7) and the 10th Chinese month ( November 7 – December 6).

## Family

This year, your family's fortune is not smooth. Although there will be good news and good things in your home, and there may be auspicious work, your fate has received some conflicting power from the Year of the Snake 2025, so you should be careful of your subordinates causing trouble and suffering. You should also be more careful about safety in your home, especially paying close attention to the health of the elderly. Most importantly, you must be careful about your behavior. Do not show off or act more prominent than others. Also, be careful not to speak to intimidate or criticize others because there are people who are not happy. Be careful that you will unknowingly encounter danger. The months that you should be more careful are the 4th Chinese month (May 5 – June 4), the 5th

Chinese month (June 5 – July 6), the 9th Chinese month (October 8 – November 6), and the 11th Chinese month (December 7, 2025 – January 4, 2026). Be careful of conflicts that turn small matters into big ones. Be careful of accidents both inside and outside the home. You should also be careful of criminals. You should also not get involved in conflicts between friends. Sometimes it's better to just ignore it when something happens and it causes trouble for the people at home.

**Love**

This year, the love life of the person is quite unstable. There are always arguments and conflicts. For those who do not have a partner, this year is another opportunity to have a partner. However, due to the influence of the Mara Tao Hua star, it means that the love you encounter will be temporary and will pass away. You may find love with the other person at night entertainment venues. The chances of becoming a real partner are very low and should not be chosen. For some people who already have a partner but are attracted to someone in an entertainment venue, it will lead to arguments with the real person at home. In particular, the months when your love life will experience problems and arguments are easy are the 4th Chinese month (May 5 – June 4), the 5th Chinese month (June 5 – July 6), the 9th Chinese month (October 8 – November 6), and the 11th Chinese month (December 7, 2025 – January 4, 2026). During these times, you should be mindful and firm. Be careful of your behavior and do not let small matters undermine big matters. Also, you should not get involved in other people's families. Avoid going to entertainment venues, which can lead to illnesses and problems.

## Health

The health of this person in this age group is not very good. Be careful of allergies, headaches, gastritis, enteritis, and other infectious diseases, and stress accumulation along with insufficient rest can cause illnesses. In addition, you should be more careful of accidents while traveling, especially after a party where alcohol is celebrated. You should avoid driving. In particular, the unlucky months when you should pay close attention to your health are the 4th Chinese month (May 5 – June 4), the 5th Chinese month (June 5 – July 6), the 9th Chinese month (October 8 – November 6), and the 11th Chinese month (December 7, 2025 – January 4, 2026). Be careful of accidents both while working and traveling. Be careful of sudden illnesses. Therefore, if you feel anything unusual in your body, you should see a doctor immediately for diagnosis and treatment.

**Year of the TIGER (Fire) | (1998)**
" The TIGER is on the mountain." is a person born in the year of the TIGER at the age of 27 years (1998)

**Overview**
For those born in the year of the Tiger, this year, because your birth year is classified as a clashing year with the year of the Snake (2025), another birth year, so you should not be careless in your work or activities this year. Do not be reckless or reckless. It is better to stick

to the principle of safety first. It is better than having problems and making people at home worry. If there is any auspicious event in your home this year, it will help reduce the clashing power of this year. And because the planet that moves into your horoscope house this year is the "Chiang Chae" star (warrior star), along with receiving auspicious power from the "Sam Tai" star (three sons star), which will help and support you in your work, like a chick escaping from its eggshell and having a new and bright life, it will result in you having the opportunity to be promoted, or to move, change responsibilities, or change your work location. Therefore, you should be prepared for the changes that will occur. This year, showing your superiors your work will be another way to advance in the future. Along with building and strengthening good relationships with people around you, it will also help to push you further. Enough to advance to a big position or maybe start your own business. Just be diligent in improving your skills. Success is not far from your reach. However, you should be careful of the dangers from the evil stars "Suay Pua" (the planet of danger) and "Tiew Kae" (the star of the funeral guest) that are orbiting to harass together. Therefore, you cannot be careless and complacent about accidents both during work and travel. You should be careful of injuries from arguments or being accidentally hit and suffering instead of others. Therefore, people born in the year of the Tiger at this age should find time to worship and ward off bad luck and entrust their fate to the god Tai Sui at the beginning of the year to help ease and lighten bad luck and promote smooth work and finances, and bring peace and tranquility to your life.

## Career and Business

This year's career is considered a pioneering year. Therefore, determination and diligence today will be an important foundation for future advancement. You should always make friends and strengthen your relationships with people around you who you have to contact. If you work in an organization or agency, this year you should show your skills and create work that is evident to people around you because the direction of your career and trade is bright. You are likely to be considered by your boss for a higher position. Otherwise, you will become a representative of the community of the province or a project leader with more responsibilities. The months in which your work or business will move in a prosperous direction are the 2nd Chinese month (March 5 – April 3), the 6th Chinese month (July 7 – August 6), the 8th Chinese month (September 7 – October 7), and the 10th Chinese month (November 7 – December 6). However, if you are in the following unsupportive months, you should be more careful, which are the 4th Chinese month (May 5 – June 4), the 5th Chinese month (June 5 – July 6), the 9th Chinese month (October 8 – November 6), and the 11th Chinese month (December 7, 2025 – January 4, 2026). When signing a work contract, you should consider it carefully so that there will be no problems later. You should be careful with some activities because you may be tricked into being a scapegoat. Also, you should not invest in shares during the aforementioned periods because there may be accounting fraud by the partners.

## Financial

The financial fortune of those born in the Year of the Tiger during this life is considered moderate. Income from salary or business will continue to flow in as usual. However, if you expect money from gambling, there is still a high risk. In addition, some periods of the year will face the problem of cash flow and liquidity. Therefore, if you can save anything, please save and save it early. The months when your finances will be stuck and unexpected expenses may occur are the 4th Chinese month (May 5 - June 4), the 5th Chinese month (June 5 - July 6), the 9th Chinese month (October 8 - November 6), and the 11th Chinese month (December 7, 2025 - January 4, 2026). Do not lend money to others, do not sign financial guarantees, do not gamble, do not sell illegal or copyrighted goods. Be careful, there will be problems that will drag down your finances and make you illiquid. The months when your finances will flow smoothly are the 2nd Chinese month (5 March – 3 April), the 6th Chinese month (7 July – 6 August), the 8th Chinese month (7 September – 7 October) and the 10th Chinese month (7 November – 6 December).

## Family

This year, your family's events are not good. The first thing to consider is to be careful and check the safety of your home, including equipment, tools, and appliances that are broken. They should be repaired or replaced. In addition, you should not neglect the health of the elderly in your home. However, if you have the opportunity to organize an auspicious event in your home this year, the auspicious energy will help reduce the inauspicious energy. In addition, you should make merit and worship Tai Sui to avert misfortune. The merit will help reduce the misfortunes that will occur to your family members. However, you should still be careful of the bad months and your family will face problems and chaos, which are the 4th Chinese month (May 5 - June 4), the 5th Chinese month (June 5 - July 6), the 9th Chinese month (October 8 - November 6), and the 11th

Chinese month (December 7, 2025 - January 4, 2026). Be careful of accidents in the home and be careful of dangers from criminals. In addition, you should stay away from relatives or friends who like to party or like to drink. Be careful of gatherings that will cause misfortunes. You should not interfere in your friends' conflicts because it may become a problem that will harass you.

**Love**

This year, your love will face some ups and downs. In terms of love, today you should consider your readiness carefully. If you are not ready and do not feel that it is right for you, do not force yourself to do so. However, if you find the right person and have made up your mind, you should have the courage to ask for their hand in marriage and make it official. Because if you delay it any longer, someone may try to steal them away. And since this year, the power of the Chinese chrysanthemum may cause you to become infatuated with temporary love and lose your senses. Or, you may fall in love with a service girl in an entertainment venue. You should think carefully because you may be gossiped about and talked about by others. The months when your love will have problems are the 4th Chinese month (May 5 – June 4), the 5th Chinese month (June 5 – July 6), the 9th Chinese month (October 8 – November 6), and the 11th Chinese month (December 7, 2025 – January 4, 2026). You should not go to entertainment venues that sell services. If your lover is a good person, you must be steadfast and visit them often. Be careful, misunderstandings can lead to arguments that can shatter your relationship.

**Health**

This year, the overall health of the person is in good condition. However, due to the appearance of a bad start in the health base, it will spread its influence and cause bad results in accidents to the point of bloodshed. Therefore, during work and traveling both near and far, do not be careless. Be careful that you may encounter bloodshed and cause worries to your family members. The months that you must be especially careful and pay more attention to are the 4th Chinese month (May 5 – June 4), the 5th Chinese month (June 5 – July 6), the 9th Chinese month (October 8 – November 6), and the 11th Chinese month (December 7, 2025 – January 4, 2026). During these times, do not be quick-tempered, do not believe others, act on impulse, or lose control of your temper, or you will respond to the other party with an eye for an eye or a tooth for a tooth. In the end, both parties will be damaged and hurt.

## Chinese Astrology Horoscope for Each Month

## Month 12 in the Dragon Year (5 Jan 25 - 2 Feb 25)

The horoscope of those born in the year of the Tiger has improved a lot this month, but it still cannot escape the shadow of misfortune, causing both good and bad things to occur. In terms of work and business, there will be obstacles that make work more difficult. You may need to rely on your interpersonal skills to help. Also, when signing various contracts, you still need to consider them carefully. What you should do this month is to consider others' feelings. Doing good and being kind to others will give you good opportunities in return. However, it is not that if someone does you bad things, you will do bad things back. Instead, you should treat anyone who does you bad things and do good things in return, which will stop the vengefulness. In addition, you should quickly solve the problems that are still pending with those close to you.

As for your finances this month, they are moderate. Since your income is stable, you should not add burdens to yourself and your family by spending money on gambling because gambling will both win and lose. During this time, you should be careful of unexpected expenses from those who are underlings or close subordinates. Starting a new job or investing in various things, this month is fairly smooth.

In terms of your family, you need to be careful of the health of your family members, whether they are young children or the elderly. Be careful that carelessness will cause unexpected accidents. Relatives and friends are good and will help you.

As for your health, it is fairly good. Just be careful about drinking alcohol and eating unhygienic food, it will affect you and cost you money to take care of it.

For love, during this time, the waves are calm. You should find time to relax with your partner or lover to change the atmosphere. It will help to relieve the knots in your heart and help strengthen your relationship.

**Support Days**:  1 Jan., 5 Jan., 9 Jan., 13 Jan., 17 Jan., 21 Jan., 25 Jan., 29 Jan.
**Lucky Days**: 6 Jan., 18 Jan., 30 Jan.
**Misfortune Days:** 3 Jan., 15 Jan., 27 Jan.
**Bad Days:** 12 Jan., 24 Jan.

## Month 1 in the Snake Year (3 Feb 25 - 4 Mar 25)

This month, your horoscope shows many bad stars targeting you. In terms of work, you should be careful about communicating with your subordinates or subordinates. Be careful that there will be mistakes that cause trouble. You should also be careful about personal problems in protests or abandoning work, which will cause damage. In such a situation, it is easy for small matters to escalate into big issues, which will worsen your work problems and make them more complicated. The solution is that you must pay attention to your subordinates and learn to build relationships by putting yourself in their shoes. If you use your power more than your kindness in the long run, you will fail.

This month, your finances are in the middle range. Your income is stable. However, money from luck is at high risk of loss. Therefore, do not hope for too much so that you do not lose your money. As for investments, you should postpone them for now.

This month, your family is in a situation where things are lost. You must be more careful and keep your valuables safe. You must be careful of thieves and pay more attention to the safety of your family members. Sharp objects or objects that are at risk of causing harm and are flammable must be kept in their proper place. Your love life during this period is not as you wish. Be careful about going to entertainment venues that may lead to problems and arguments with your family members. For relatives, there will be an opportunity to travel far together to do public service or go on a trip together.

Your health is good. Just be careful of food poisoning. Therefore, you should eat freshly cooked food.

**Support Days**: 2 Feb., 6 Feb., 10 Feb., 14 Feb., 18 Feb., 22 Feb., 26 Feb.
**Lucky Days**: 2 Feb., 6 Feb.
**Misfortune Days:** 8 Feb., 20 Feb.
**Bad Days:** 5 Feb., 17 Feb.

## Month 2 in the Snake Year (3 Mar 25 - 5 Apr 25)

This month, the horoscope of those born in the year of the Tiger has passed the monsoon and the auspicious star shines brightly above the horoscope, which has a positive effect on your life during this period. This will make your career and business directions find a path of progress. The assigned projects will be able to be pushed through to completion. The problems that you used to have will be reduced. Obstacles will find supporters to help. This is a good opportunity to create work or increase sales. Therefore, you must use this opportunity to add new skills and knowledge. Always be prepared. If you see a good opportunity, what you hope for will come to your hands.

This month, finances are abundant. There will be income flowing in from many sources. However, you should weigh the situation carefully. As for taking risks hoping for unexpected windfalls or stock lottery, you have a chance to win a lot of money.

During this period, the family is peaceful. The atmosphere in the house is bright. Members love each other and are happy and full of smiles. When the energy in the house is smooth, it will result in good results for work outside the home. As for relatives, they will find support and help.

As for the health horoscope during this period, even though you are getting better, those who have chronic diseases or chronic diseases during this period will have the opportunity to see a good doctor with good medicine to help cure your symptoms. However, you still cannot be careless about accidents both during work and travel. Be careful that during this period there is a possibility of accidents that cause bleeding.

In terms of love, this period is another month with good times for asking for a proposal, getting engaged, or getting married. If you are in love, you should be open and dare to speak. Don't wait, otherwise you may regret it.

**Support Days**: 2 Mar, 6 Mar., 10 Mar., 14 Mar., 18 Mar., 22 Mar., 26 Mar., 30 Mar.
**Lucky Days**: 7 Mar, 19 Mar., 31 Mar.
**Misfortune Days:** 4 Mar, 16 Mar., 28 Mar.
**Bad Days:** 1 Mar, 13 Mar., 25 Mar.

**Month 3 in the Snake Year (4 Apr 25 - 4 May 25)**
For those born in the year of the Tiger, even though this year is a year of conflict, you don't need to be overly afraid. If you have a strong will and are determined to be careful, you will be able to get through it. At the beginning of this year, if you have time, you should go and pay respect to Tai Sui to enhance your auspiciousness and escape from disasters. Then, you should allocate your budget for the whole year to set your direction and goals.

Because your overall horoscope this month is not very good, both in terms of work and business, there are still many problems to think about during this period. Therefore, you should consider every activity carefully. When signing any contract, you should think carefully. Do not make rash decisions. Find information from all sides beforehand so that you do not regret it later.

For your work during this period, even though you encounter many obstacles, use your wisdom to solve them. Do not be patient and let a big problem become a crisis on top of a crisis. This month, what you should do is visit your elders, customers, business partners, and people you have to contact. You should avoid investing because there is a chance that you will get hurt and be cheated.

Your finances during this period will encounter a storm. Income is low but expenses are high. Therefore, you should manage your money to balance it well from the beginning. Refrain from gambling and taking risks. Avoid lending money to others and acting as a guarantor for others.

There is nothing to worry about in your family. If there are any problems, they can be solved.

As for your health, it is not good. You will get sick easily. Be careful of old diseases recurring and be careful of hidden diseases. The hygiene of the elderly should always be kept clean and you should pay close attention to them. As for you, you must be careful of getting injured in accidents both while working and traveling.

In terms of love, there are still some problems. You must be firm and avoid going to entertainment venues with service girls because you may catch a disease.

**Support Days**: 3 Apr., 7 Apr., 11 Apr., 15 Apr., 19 Apr., 23 Apr., 27 Apr.
**Lucky Days**: 12 Apr., 24 Apr.
**Misfortune Days:** 9 Apr., 21 Apr.
**Bad Days:** 6 Apr., 18 Apr., 30 Apr.

**Month 4 in the Snake Year (5 May 25 - 4 Jun 25)**
This month, your life path will encounter many bad stars orbiting in your horoscope. This will result in unexpected events in your family and you will often encounter problems with unimportant matters that cause chaos and trouble. What you should do this month is to ease the burden and take care of family harmony. Many problems should be discussed with people in the house so that decisions will not be wrong.

As for your finances, you will be in a position of losing wealth. Even though your income is good, there will be unexpected expenses that will drain your money, causing a lack of liquidity. Therefore, during this period, you must avoid unnecessary extravagance. Do not gamble in any form and do not be greedy in the hope of getting rich quickly by doing illegal business because you have a chance of being sued and punished criminally.

As for your work and business, this period will encounter storms. Those who work regularly during this period should be careful of job changes and it will affect your future career. Therefore, you should take care of your responsibilities as best you can. You must be more careful when doing various work activities and planning. Always develop new skills to keep up with changes.

In terms of your family, this period lacks peace. Be careful of the safety and illness of your family members. Especially the elders in the house who may have to spend money on medical expenses.

Love's horoscope during this period is moderate. You may have to spend more time with each other. As for working together or investing, you should refrain from doing so for safety reasons.

Health during this period is not so good. You should be careful of liver disease, high blood pressure, food poisoning, and stress accumulation will cause illnesses to manifest during this period.

**Support Days**:  1 May, 5 May, 9 May, 13 May, 17 May, 21 May, 25 May, 29 May.
**Lucky Days**: 6 May, 18 May, 30 May.
**Misfortune Days:** 3 May, 15 May, 27 May.
**Bad Days:** 12 May, 24 May.


**Month 5 in the Snake Year (5 Jun 25 - 6 Jul 25)**
This month, your horoscope for those born in the year of the Tiger, whether you move forward or backward, will face difficulties because there will be bad stars surrounding your horoscope, which will cause problems, both conflicts between individuals, subordinates, or subordinates causing trouble, unexpected expenses, and accounting and tax problems that will cause cash flow to disappear from liquidity. For your work and business, this period will encounter challenges. If you do not change your plan to accept newcomers or fix past weaknesses, it will be difficult to withstand the situation. Also, if you find a problem, you should fix it immediately. Do not let it spread until it is difficult to fix. Be more careful when signing a work contract. Do not

sign because you are being insulted or provoked.

This month, your direct income will not be spectacular. As for money from luck, there will be some. However, if you are not careful when taking risks in various aspects, you will have a higher chance of losing than gaining. Importantly, during this period, you should not lend money to others or be a guarantor for anyone. Do not invest in businesses that are at risk of being illegal. You should save up money in advance to fix emergencies. Investments are not good, there is a chance of being cheated.

For your family horoscope, there is no peace. Be careful of subordinates causing trouble. Be careful of accidents with family members. Beware of scammers

In terms of sweet love, it is suitable to take your partner on a vacation. It is an opportunity to increase intimacy and create more bonds.

**Support Days**: 2 Jun., 6 Jun., 10 Jun., 14 Jun., 18 Jun., 22 Jun., 26 Jun., 30 Jun.
**Lucky Days**: 11 Jun., 23 Jun.
**Misfortune Days:** 8 Jun., 20 Jun.
**Bad Days:** 5 Jun., 17 Jun. 29 Jun.

## Month 6 in the Snake Year (7 Jul 25 - 6 Aug 25)

Your horoscope has passed the obstacles and has moved into a suitable month. In addition, auspicious stars are shining, which creates a supportive force that helps and promotes your horoscope, allowing your work or business to move forward to its goal of prosperity once again. Therefore, what you should do this month is to know how to seize this good opportunity and work hard to your full potential, create results, and increase sales without paying attention to objections. Do not let this good opportunity pass you by in vain. In addition, you must have the courage to resolve conflicts within your organization by remaining neutral and fair. If it is right, say it is right, if it is wrong, say it is wrong, and dare to speak up. Then the organization will finally move forward.

This month, your fortune and finances are quite good. Direct income is normal, but money from gambling should be limited because if you are greedy and do not stop, you may be taken back.

In terms of work, this period is obstructed. You will find a sponsor. Your work will increase, but you should not be engrossed or arrogant with praise. Instead, you should be diligent in increasing your knowledge and new skills. Then you will see the numbers in your account increase as you wish. For those who are looking for various investment channels, This period has a bright future, it can be done.

For a peaceful family, parents and children help each other and fill each other with love and encouragement.

However, in terms of health, you must be extra careful, especially if you do not get enough rest and eat whatever you want, which will cause other diseases to flare up and may reduce your energy to create work and hinder your progress.

For love, it is in good condition, there is a chance to meet the right person.

**Support Days**:  4 Jul., 8 Jul., 12 Jul., 16 Jul., 20 Jul., 24 Jul., 28 Jul., 29 Jul.
**Lucky Days**: 5 Jul., 17 Jul., 29 Jul.
**Misfortune Days:** 2 Jul., 14 Jul., 26 Jul.
**Bad Days:** 11 Jul., 23 Jul.

## Month 7 in the Snake Year (7 Aug 25 - 6 Sep 25)

Entering this month, for the Tiger zodiac sign, even though the career direction is improving, there are still conflicts in the management line, which are obstacles to work. Therefore, what will help is fairness. When expressing opinions or making decisions on any matter, you must be neutral, and reasonable, and know how to compromise. The work of the group will then progress. Importantly, do not interfere with the work of others, and should not look for faults or do things beyond your authority.

For this salary, direct income is passable. And may see some money from windfalls, but should not be greedy. When you get it, you should know when to stop and when to stop, so that it will not be damaged. During this time, if there is money left, you can invest more in gold and keep it.

In terms of work, you will meet someone who will help you. You should increase your diligence to create results and expand your income. You should also try to find ways to reduce conflicts in the department.

The family is peaceful and receives auspicious energy. There will be good news about the success of people in the family. Otherwise, there will be a new little member in the family. As for relatives, be careful of your behavior and words. When you say anything, you must think about the other person's feelings. If you are not careful, it may harm your work and relationships.

Love is smooth. During this time, your lover will take care of you, spoil you, and pay attention to you without being far away.

For your health, there will be no serious illnesses to worry about.

**Support Days**: 1 Aug., 5 Aug., 9 Aug., 13 Aug., 17 Aug., 21 Aug., 25 Aug., 29 Aug.
**Lucky Days**: 10 Aug., 22 Aug.
**Misfortune Days:** 7 Aug., 19 Aug., 31 Aug.
**Bad Days:** 4 Aug., 16 Aug., 28 Aug.


**Month 8 in the Snake Year (7 Sep 25 - 7 Oct 25)**
This month, the horoscope of those born in the year of the Tiger is still in a good direction. Your career and business will find a new path of progress. Just wait for you to decide to take action and step towards your goal. Your career and business will meet a patron who will help guide you and solve problems. You can increase your work and expand your business, resulting in progress and prosperity. Therefore, what you should do this month is to be diligent in creating work and making sales to compensate for the past rough times. Your income will increase quite a bit.

For financial luck, during this period, there will be a fair amount of income from your main job. There is also a good opportunity to expand your income in special work or money from various brokerage fees, including short-term investments in various fields. There is some windfall profit. If you think of taking risks and speculating, you will receive some money, but do not be greedy or your fortune will disappear.

Within your family, the situation will ease the tension and you may receive good news about the success of your family members. You may have a chance to move, such as moving to a new house or workplace, or you may have to work in a distant land and may buy expensive property for your home.

In terms of health, your body is strong. Relatives and friends will help you, including opportunities to work together in business. Love is in a state of tension, leading to a cold war between you. Be careful of arguments arising from small matters. You should spend more time paying attention to your partner and avoid going to entertainment venues.

**Support Days**: 2 Sep, 6 Sep., 10 Sep., 14 Sep., 18 Sep., 22 Sep., 26 Sep., 30 Sep.
**Lucky Days**: 3 Sep, 15 Sep., 27 Sep.
**Misfortune Days:** 12 Sep, 24 Sep.
**Bad Days:** 9 Sep, 21 Sep.

**Month 9 in the Snake Year (8 Oct 25 - 6 Nov 25)**
This month, your life path is moving to a conflicting line, causing many things that are currently in progress to come to a halt, experiencing unevenness. The direction of your destiny tends to continue to fall. What you should do on this occasion to protect yourself from danger is that all work activities must use patience to overcome. Sometimes you may have to know how to protect yourself by not interfering with the responsibilities of others. At the beginning of the month, you should find time to worship the Buddha and make merit to ask for their blessing to help ease the burden of becoming light.

This month, your finances are in a state of losing money. You should not gamble or take risks. Do not lend money to others or be a financial guarantee. Do not get involved or invest in illegal businesses, including products that infringe copyrights.

In terms of work, you will encounter obstacles. You should be careful about communicating with others, as it will result in work that is different from the goal. In some matters, you may have to use your human relations skills to resolve the situation. As for various investments, during this period, if you do not want to stop, you should choose the ones with the least risk to maintain the reserve funds in the system. Collaboration and investment are not good.

This period is not peaceful within the family. This is another month that you have to be careful about valuables being lost or stolen. Beware of illnesses of family members, including mourning for elders.

In terms of love, there will be conflicts and disagreements every day. You should be patient and calm.

In terms of health, unexpected events may occur, causing injuries to the point of hospitalization. You should be mindful of everything you do and be careful when traveling long distances.

**Support Days**:  7 Oct., 10 Oct., 11 Oct., 19 Oct., 22 Oct., 23 Oct., 31 Oct.
**Lucky Days**: 9 Oct., 21 Oct., 2 Oct.
**Misfortune Days:** 12 Oct., 15 Oct., 24 Oct., 27 Oct.
**Bad Days:** 6 Oct., 8 Oct., 18 Oct., 20 Oct., 30 Oct., 1 Oct.

**Month 10 in the Snake Year (7 Nov 25 - 6 Dec 25)**
This month, your horoscope for those born in the Year of the Tiger seems to have passed a critical point. Many auspicious stars are orbiting to shine and help. This results in many things that you expect and intend to adjust in a better direction. Both in terms of finance and work, you will find someone to help you, making problems and obstacles lighter. It is also a time of prosperity. Therefore, you should seize this good opportunity to quickly expand and find ways to create work, increase sales, or find new business channels. This will help strengthen the old foundation and help expand your income. If you work hard, your work and income will be impressive. What you should do this month is to clear up old problems that have been piling up and finish them while moving forward with new work. Don't let them become a burden for the future. During this period, you can wait for the right time and then fully move forward with the projects that you had planned.

Your financial fortune will flourish according to your career horoscope. You will have the opportunity to receive wealth from many channels, whether it is your current regular income, income from things you have invested and worked hard for, or you will also see unexpected windfalls. However, you should be careful not to spend too much or your money may bounce back into the red. Joint ventures, starting new jobs, and various small investments Fairly smoothly, will make a profit.

Within the family, there is peace, love is smooth and sweet. This period is considered another auspicious time for some couples who have spent time studying each other until they are ripe. There is an engagement, marriage, or childbirth.

Health should be careful of high blood pressure, heart disease, and liver disease and be more careful about accidents while traveling.

**Support Days**: 1 Nov., 5 Nov., 9 Nov., 13 Nov., 17 Nov., 21 Nov., 25 Nov ., 29 Nov.
**Lucky Days**: 2 Nov., 14 Nov., 26 Nov.
**Misfortune Days**: 11 Nov., 23 Nov.

**Bad Days:** 8 Nov., 20 Nov.

## Month 11 in the Snake Year (7 Dec 25 - 4 Jan 26)

This month, your horoscope is moving towards both love and hate. In addition, in your horoscope house, there are two groups of bad stars orbiting together, which will affect the loss of a large sum of money and unexpected events. Your work and business are often stuck and have problems. However, you should quickly solve them and not let the problems drag on until they are difficult to fix. The important thing during this period is that you should handle your work with mindfulness and avoid the causes that will cause conflict. This is another month that you should take good care of your work and responsibilities. During this period, you should be more careful about making contracts and be careful not to be cheated or taken advantage of. In terms of money, this month, your income is low, but your expenses are overwhelming. Being frugal and saving will help you relieve the problem.

In terms of windfall profits, it is not good. Investing in risky stocks and speculating in various fields should be avoided for now. Do not invest in risky businesses and avoid lending money to others.

In terms of family, the situation has not yet been resolved. Holding on to stubbornness and wanting to win against people in the house is not the answer. In addition, do not overlook the safety of people in the house. Items that may be dangerous must be stored neatly. You must be careful of unexpected events, especially the elders in the house. Both should be careful of scammers. As for close friends and relatives, this month you may have to keep your distance because there will be troubles that will bother you continuously.

As for physical and mental health, this period is not very good. Be careful of stomach diseases, and liver diseases. Also, when traveling on the road during this period, do not be careless. It is easy to have an accident. Do not drink alcohol while driving or drive drunk.

In terms of love, it is still stable. Even though there are some conflicts due to emotions, it is considered that we can still talk about it. It is not a big problem.

**Support Days**:  3 Dec., 7 Dec., 11 Dec., 15 Dec., 19 Dec., 23 Dec., 27 Dec., 31 Dec.
**Lucky Days**: 8 Dec., 20 Dec.
**Misfortune Days:** 5 Dec., 17 Dec., 29 Dec.
**Bad Days:** 2 Dec., 14 Dec., 26 Dec.

## Amulet for The Year of the TIGER
## "Dharma Master Tang Sanzang"

Those born in the Year of the Tiger this year should set up and worship the sacred object "Phra Dharma Master Tang Sanzang" to enhance their destiny. Place it on your work desk or cash desk to ask for his power and authority to protect you from dangers, as well as help solve problems, obstacles, and disasters, eliminate and relieve the person of the horoscope from suffering and all kinds of troubles, and create only fortune, wealth and auspicious things throughout the year.

In one chapter of the Advanced Feng Shui, it was mentioned the deities who will come down to reside in the Mie Keng (House of Destiny) of the year, which are deities who can bring both good and bad things to the person of the horoscope of that year. Therefore, worshiping to enhance your destiny with the deity who comes down to reside in the year of your birth is considered to have the best results and have the most impact on you. This is to rely on the power of that deity to help protect you while your destiny is declining and having bad karma to reduce it. At the same time, ask for his blessing to help inspire your business and trade to go smoothly as desired, and bring glory and prosperity to you and your family.

Those born in the year of the Tiger or Mie Keng (horoscope house) in the zodiac sign of the Yang, when coming to the year of the Snake, will be classified as another zodiac sign of the clashing year. Therefore, bad energy will cover the horoscope house. In addition, there will be the evil star "Tiew Kae" (funeral guest star) and the inauspicious star "Kuang Chi" (tongue-rolling star) orbiting to cause trouble. Which will result in the results in terms of a career that will not be worth the sweat you have put in. There will be conflicts and arguments easily. Work and business will be full of problems and chaos. It cannot be taken care of all at once. Also, subordinates will cause trouble. Therefore, for every activity this year, you should look carefully before doing it. Also, you should not interfere in the work of others. Also, be careful of unexpected changes that you should not be careless about. In terms of luck, your luck will decrease this year. Income is low. Expenses are fast. You should avoid gambling and speculation for your happiness. This year, it seems difficult to find true love. As for love, your health is good, but after May, it may get worse. You should take care of your hygiene in terms of food and be careful of getting sick with liver disease. In addition, more attention should be paid to the safety and health of family members who are likely to suffer from bloodshed, including unexpected events related to mourning for elders. However, since the auspicious star "Tian Yi" is orbiting to help, it will alleviate some of the burden. At the beginning of the year, for many things to go smoothly, those born in the Year of the Tiger should find time to pay homage and ask for blessings from Tai Sui to avert misfortune and alleviate disasters.

In addition, if you think of solving or eliminating bad events, you should establish and worship "Phra Dharma Master Tang

Sanzang" to ask for his power and authority to help eliminate and dispel misfortunes, resolve the destructive power of the evil star, and help promote the owner's career and business to flourish and progress, with smooth circulation of goods, abundant fortune, and good health and a safe and happy family. "Phra Dharma Master Tang Sanzang", originally named "Xianzang, Surname Tan", is from Henan Province, China. He was a natural genius. He was someone who had been studying the Dharma since he was young. When he grew up, he became a monk and became famous for his morality, concentration, and wisdom. He was supported by Emperor Tang Taizong, the first emperor of the Tang Dynasty. Emperor Tang Taizong was a person who highly believed in Buddhism and also loved and respected Venerable Hian Zhang, so he made him his adopted younger brother. Venerable Hian Zhang was a diligent monk who devoted his life to worshiping the Buddha.

He studied, researched, and collected the true teachings of Buddhism. He traveled from China to the remote and rugged land of Jambudvipa for 19 years, covering a distance of more than 50,000 li. He was determined to spread Buddhism and collect the Tripitaka, which was of great benefit to Buddhists all over the world. He was therefore given the name "Tang Sanzang", which means "Tripitaka". The Chinese called him "Tang Sanzang Huabsi", which means "The Dharma Master who translated the Tripitaka in the Tang Dynasty". Worshiping the Buddha will help eliminate misfortunes and end all misfortunes and sorrows. No evil people to cause trouble, and find a convenient and bright path in doing business and various duties, and help everything go smoothly as desired and have everything to be complete.

In addition, those born in the Year of the Tiger should wear a lucky pendant of "Phra Dharma Master Tang Sanzang" around their neck or carry it with them when traveling outside the home, whether near or far, so that the person will be filled with auspicious wealth, have prosperity and progress in both business and trade and have a peaceful and happy family throughout the year, resulting in better and faster efficiency than before.

**Good Direction:** Northeast, Northwest, and South
**Bad Direction:** North
**Lucky Colors**: Green, Blue, Gray, Black, and Blue.
**Lucky Times:** 11.00 – 11.59, 19.00 – 20.59, 21.00 – 22.59.
**Bad Times:** 09.00 – 10.59, 15.00 – 16.59, 23.00 – 00.59.

# Good Luck
# For
# 2025